HIM & HER'S
DAY OF
THE DEAL

PAR WILSON

WRITTEN & DRAWN BY	CRIME CONSULTANCY BY	ART ASSISTANCE BY	PUBLISHED BY
JASON WILSON	TONY SPENCER	TERRY JONES	DEALER COMICS

*This first edition first published in Great Britain by
Dealer Comics.*

*Printed in Great Britain
www.smugglingvacation.co.uk*

ISBN 978-0-9559170-1-1

AAAH! ALLEYTON. THAT SMALL STUBBORN INDUSTRIAL TOWN THAT PUNCHED ABOVE ITS WEIGHT FOR SO LONG; THE HOME OF OUR TRIO OF FAILED SMUGGLERS - STAN, KAYE AND MIKEY...

SO WHAT WAS THE FALLOUT FROM THE WHOLE SMUGGLING VACATION FIASCO?

PASTILLE JONES FINALLY RETRIEVED HIS GEAR AND RETURNED TO SPAIN...

THAT'S TWO HUNDRED AND TWENTY GRAND EXACTLY!

GOOD - BAG IT UP FOR LATER.

...WHERE BUSINESS SOON RETURNED TO NORMAL.

HIS WORKERS MINSTREL, POLO, TREBOR AND SMARTY RETURNED TO A ROUTINE OF WORK AND PLAY...

WOW! FUCK! LOOK AT HER MATE...

THAT'S A TEN.

...BIT SKINNY FOR ME.

...NEVER WORKING TOO HARD.

DRUGDEALER AND NIGHTCLUB OWNER BROWNIE PRICE OPENED HIS FIRST CASINO...

YOU'RE SUCH A CLEVER MAN YOU ARE?

I KNOW.

WHO SAYS CRIME DOESN'T PAY?

-AND LOCAL DEALER 'ROO'? HE CARRIES ON AWAITING THE DAY WHEN BROWNIE GRANTS HIM A BREAK INTO THE BIG TIME.

THIRD YEAR AT THIS... SHOULD BE A MILLIONAIRE BY NOW! LIFE'S SO FUCKING UNFAIR.

AS FOR OUR FAILED TRIO OF SMUGGLERS...MIKEY RETURNED TO HIS LIFE OF HARD WORK...

...ANOTHER PINT PLEASE LOVE.

KAYE RETURNS TO HER JOB AT MARKS AND SPENCERS WHERE HER PATIENCE IS A VIRTUE...

COULD YOU JUST MAKE UP YOUR MIND!! I DO HAVE THINGS TO DO YOU KNOW!

CHANGING ROOMS

AND STAN? STAN RETURNS TO THE I.T JOB HE ADORES SO MUCH...

YOU'VE GOT TWO MINUTES! THEN I'M GONNA SMASH YOUR FUCKING... ...BLOODY...STUPID...GNNRR!!

ALL SEEMS TO HAVE RETURNED TO NORMAL...OR HAS IT?

THEY STRIP DOWN AND GLOVE UP...

YOU CAN START DOWN THAT END...I'LL START DOWN HERE.

ALRIGHT. LET'S CRACK ON...

THEY GO THROUGH THE USUAL PROCESS OF MAINTAINING FOOD, WATER AND P.H LEVELS AS WELL AS CHECKING THE HEALTH OF THE PLANTS...

SIGNS OF BUD ROT ON THIS ONE - THAT'S THE THIRD ONE!

MAKE A NOTE OF WHEREABOUTS AND WE'LL TELL MIKEY LATER ON.

HE SHOULD HAVE SPOTTED THIS HIMSELF! HE HAS BEEN BY HERE THIS WEEK HASN'T HE?

COURSE HE HAS. I THINK HE MUST JUST HAVE OTHER THINGS ON HIS MIND AT THE MOMENT.

SUCH AS WHAT FOR INSTANCE?

SUCH AS...

ALLEYTON LIBRARY: CENTRE OF LEARNING FOR MANY, BOTH YOUNG AND OLD...

THOUGH FOR ONE YOUNG MAN, THE LIBRARY IS NOT JUST A PLACE OF LEARNING...

...IT IS ALSO A PLACE TO HUNT WOMEN! OR RATHER — ONE WOMAN IN PARTICULAR...

THESE'LL DO THE JOB. SHE'LL BE DEAD IMPRESSED!

LIKE A LION HE WAITS...

WATCHING...

...incessant small talk ...natter...gossip... ...pointless chat...

PATIENTLY STALKING HIS PREY...

HURRY UP FOR FUCK'S SAKE! YOU WON'T READ 'EM ALL ANYWAY.

AT LAST! THE COAST IS CLEAR...

BYE THEN.

SEE YA.

IN HE GOES...

ALRIGHT JEN, HOW'S THINGS?

...MORNIN' MIKEY. BACK AGAIN SO SOON?

YEAH — JUST A FEW FOR THE WEEKEND. BIT OF HISTORY AND THAT.

SO WHAT DO YOU HAVE THIS TIME..?

...A CENTURY OF THE MAFIA...INTERESTING CHOICE...

AND THIS ONE ON NAPOLEON. I REMEMBER YOU SAYING HOW MUCH YOU RATED IT.

AAAH — GOOD CHOICE. I'M SURE YOU'LL ENJOY IT.

...SO WHAT YOU UP TO THIS WEEKEND..?

NOT SURE...BOOKS TO CATCH UP ON... SOME PAINTING TO DO. YOU'LL BE DOWN THE 'LION' I'M GUESSING.

TAP! TAP! TAP!

AT THE LION.

...SAYS HE'S GOT A FEW THINGS ON THE GO THAT MIGHT TIDE US OVER.

WELL HE'D BEST HURRY UP—BEFORE OUR GAS & ELECTRIC GET'S CUT OFF!

NO WORRIES. I'LL HAVE A WORD.

YOU JUST DO THAT.

RIGHT. I'M GETTING MYSELF A BEER & SOME GRUB. WHAT ABOUT YOU?

sigh...I'M NOT HUNGRY. JUST GET ME ANOTHER WINE.

ALRIGHT COZ.

ALRIGHT STAN. YOU SEEN THE PAPER?

YEAH. ANOTHER HUNDRED LAYED OFF. THE WAY THINGS ARE GOING WE'LL ALL BE OUT OF WORK BEFORE YOU...

NO, NO. NOT THE LOCAL. I'M ON ABOUT THE BIRMINGHAM PAPER. LOOK—IT'S RIGHT ON THE FRONT PAGE...

LOOK SEE!

BIRMINGHAM Mail

DRUG RAID AT CASINO

80 OFFICERS INVOLVED IN SWOOP

FUCK ME! DIDN'T KNOW ANYTHING ABOUT THIS. THAT'S BROWNIE'S PLACE INNIT?

THAT'S RIGHT. ROO AND MIKEY USED TO WORK FOR HIM. WELL, HIS CASINO WAS CLOSED ALL LAST NIGHT...

WILL BE CLOSED TONIGHT AN' ALL I BET. ARRESTED LOADS THEY HAVE. EVEN PULLED IN MORGAN AND TIFF THIS MORNIN'...THEY NOT PULLED IN YOUR MIKEY THEN?

NAAH...HE DOESN'T REALLY HAVE ANYTHING TO DO WITH THE CASINO PEOPLE ANYMORE. HE WOULDN'T BE INVOLVED.

THAT'S A RELIEF! INTO A LOT OF SHIT THOSE CASINO PEOPLE. I FOR ONE, WOULDN'T HAVE ANYTHING TO DO WITH THEM STAN.

ME NEITHER—BESIDES, I SPOKE TO MIKEY LAST NIGHT AND HE WAS SOUND.

THAT'S GOOD. 'CAUSE HE DON'T WANT TO GET INVOLVED IN ALL THAT SHIT. REAL HEAVY STUFF.

THE LOCAL REC...

SO HOW THE FUCK DID THEY MISS IT?

JUST BAD TIMING REALLY.

'WAS SUPPOSED TO ARRIVE IN WEDNESDAY NIGHT. GOT DELAYED BY FRENCH STRIKES OR SOMETHING. COME YESTERDAY, THE OLD BILL GO IN FULL FORCE WHEN SOME DELIVERY VAN ARRIVES IN AND FIND FUCK ALL!

AND WHAT ABOUT CASINO GUY. THEY GET HIM?

NAAH! HE'D GOT OUT OUT EARLIER. RECKONS HE SPOTTED THE SURVEILLANCE.

SO WHAT DO YOU SAY?

DUNNO. IT'S A BIT HEAVY. I MEAN - THREE TON!!

C'MON MIKEY. IT'S A BIGGER QUANTITY FOR BIGGER MONEY. THEY NEED PEOPLE OFFSIDE WHO THEY CAN TRUST. WE'RE PERFECT FOR IT...

IT'S A TOUGH ONE. I COULD DO WITH THE CASH BUT THIS IS REAL HEAVY. OLD BILL'LL STILL BE ON THE JOB.

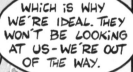

WHICH IS WHY WE'RE IDEAL. THEY WON'T BE LOOKING AT US - WE'RE OUT OF THE WAY.

...WE'RE LOW PROFILE. KNOW WHAT WE'RE DOING AND HE TRUSTS US A HUNDRED PER CENT!

THE GEAR'S COMING THROUGH ON THE BOAT RIGHT NOW. CASINO GUY'LL CALL US ONCE IT'S THROUGH AND SAFE.

SO WHEN'S THAT THEN?

ABOUT LUNCHTIME. HE'LL RING ME AS SOON AS HE KNOWS. I'LL THEN RING YOU AND WE'LL GET MOVING.

IT'LL BE ME, YOU AND TWO OTHERS. SO WHAT DO YOU SAY? YOU IN?

OLD BILL ARE GONNA BE ALL OVER THIS Y'KNOW.

DON'T WORRY ABOUT 'EM. THEY HAVEN'T GOT A FUCKING CLUE!

NOT A CLUE? HE COULD BE RIGHT...

THREE TON OF RESIN I WAS TOLD. SO WHERE THE **FUCK** IS **IT**?!!

casino ROULLETTE

POLICE

*SOCA'S OPERATION ROULETTE IS NOT GOING WELL.

LET'S GET THIS RIGHT. WE'VE BEEN FOLLOWING THIS FOR DAYS NOW, WE EVEN HAVE THE MAIN SUSPECT SAYING IT'S ARRIVED IN... ...OTHER PHONE INTERCEPTS BACK THIS UP...

WE'RE AS PUZZLED AS YOU SIR.

...SHIPMENT WAS DUE IN AT TEN. THE VEHICLE - WHICH CAME IN ON THE DOT... WAS CARRYING OFFICE FURNITURE ONLY... PLUS NO SIGN OF THE OWNER AT ALL...

HE SEEMS TO HAVE SLIPPED OUT THE BUILDING.

HOW ON EARTH A MAN IN A WHEELCHAIR CAN SLIP OUT UNDER TOP HEAVY SURVEILLENCE I DON'T KNOW... -SOMETHING'S NOT RIGHT...

...I'M THINKING THEY'VE NOTICED THE SURVEILLENCE AND PLAYED IT AS NORMAL -IN WHICH CASE OUR SHIPMENT HAS TO HAVE GONE ELSEWHERE...

QUESTION IS WHERE?

ALRIGHT THEN. COUNT ME IN. I'M UP FOR IT.

GOOD LAD. YOU WON'T REGRET THIS...

WE STICK WITH OUR OWN PEOPLE THOUGH. I'M NOT WORKING WITH NEW PEOPLE.

THAT'S AGREED. WE'LL KEEP IT SMALL & TIGHT.

RIGHT. I'LL RING BROWNIE. LET HIM KNOW YOU'RE ON BOARD... HOPE -FULLY HE CAN LET US KNOW KNOW WHEN IT'S ALL HAPPENING.

* SOCA: SERIOUS ORGANISED CRIME AGENCY.

THE COMFORT INN. JUST EIGHT MILES WEST OF ALLEYTON...

ALRIGHT ROO. SO HOW'S IT GOING?

THE 'MISSING' CASINO OWNER BROWNIE PRICE...

HE'S IN? GREAT. GOOD LAD HE IS...

WELL KEEN HE IS...

OKAY. I'LL CALL YOU AS SOON AS IT'S CONFIRMED. SHOULD BE ABOUT TWELVISH.

HE THEN RINGS HIS SUPPLIER PASTILLE JONES...

YEAH...ALL'S GOOD. NO WORRIES...WE'LL BE READY...

GOOD. JUST BE DOUBLE CAREFUL MATE. THESE PEOPLE AREN'T DAFT.

DON'T WORRY. I'LL HAVE GOOD PEOPLE ON STANDBY. WHEN'S IT DUE TO LAND HERE?

IT'S APPROACHING THE 'WATER' RIGHT NOW. ALL'S ON TIME...

AT THE LION...

THE WHITE LION

...HOW THE FUCK DID I ALLOW THIS TO HAPPEN? THIS IS A DISASTER!!

...SO I HIT THE BALL TOWARDS THE BOTTOM...

CHRIST!! I'LL NEVER HEAR THE END OF THIS.

YESSS!

PLONK!

BLIMEY STAN. YOU'VE BEEN BEAT BY A 'GIRL'.

...I'M PLAYING KAYE THEN AM I?

DID YOU SEE THAT? I POTTED IT!....OH, YOU'RE NOT BEING MOODY NOW ARE WE?

NO! I'M FINE. JUST LEAVE ME ALONE WILL YA.

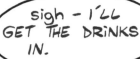

CALAIS: THE 11·40 SEA FRANCE FERRY TO DOVER, ENGLAND. H.G.V VEHICLES BOARD...

AMONGST ALL THE HAULAGE IS THE VEHICLE CARRYING THE SHIPMENT OF CANNABIS NOW HEADED FOR ALLEYTON...

...AND HERE IS THAT VEHICLE: A TYPICAL LORRY BRINGING BACK ORANGES FROM THE SOUTH OF SPAIN...

ITS DRIVER IS ALBERT ROSE, A MARRIED FATHER OF THREE WHO'S DIVERSIFIED IN RECENT YEARS.

HE'S MADE HIS PILE AND NOW SWEARS THAT THIS TRIP IS TO BE HIS LAST. HOWEVER...

NO!...IT CAN'T BE CAN IT?

...BUT IT IS! THIS TRIP'S THE THIRTEENTH ONE YOU'VE MADE.

OH CHRIST... MY LAST TRIP'S THE THIRTEENTH!!! OH. BLOODY HELL...

GOOD JOB I'M NOT THE SUSPICIOUS TYPE...MMM...IT'S JUST A NUMBER AFTER ALL.

...IT'LL BE LANDING IN THE NEXT HOUR OR SO. WE'LL GET MOVING THEN.

ALRIGHT MATE. I'M READY TO MOVE STRAIGHT OFF, JUST LET ME KNOW.

...IN THE MEANTIME GIVE SOME THOUGHT TO WHO ELSE WE CAN USE. THEY HAVE TO BE PEOPLE WE TRUST 100%.

WHAT IS IT BRUV?

...unaudible girl chatter...

...gossip...
...chatter...
...gossip...

...ERM...IT'S NOTHING.

...THERE THEY ARE. OY! YOU TWO! YOU COMIN' OVER OR WHAT?

YEAH.

SUPPOSE SO.

THIS IS MIKEY... AND THIS IS...WELL IGNORE HIM. HE'S NOT IMPORTANT.

HIYA.

HIYA.

ALRIGHT.

THIS IS JENNIE... AN OLD BEST MATE FROM SCHOOL. SHE'S JUST MOVED BACK 'ROUND HERE. WORKS LOCAL.

AAH ...INTERESTING.

YEAH... INTERESTING.

SO WHAT YOU UP TO THIS AFTERNOON?

NOT A LOT. I'VE NOTHING PLANNED.

YES YOU HAVE. THERE'S THAT JOB OF YOURS I'M HELPING YOU WITH.

THAT'S RIGHT! BUT IT WON'T BE FOR A WHILE WILL IT. SO WE'VE TIME TO SPARE.

WINK!

BUT I THOUGHT THIS JOB WAS DEAD, DEAD IMPORTANT? OH... I SEE...

SO WE'VE PLENTY OF TIME TO STOP AND RELAX FOR A BIT. ALRIGHT?

I'LL GET THE DRINKS IN SHALL I? YOU CAN COME AND HELP ME BRUV.

OKAY. IF YOU INSIST.

SHOVE!

RETURNING FROM THE BAR...

GOT YOU THE BEST CHEAP BOTTLE THEY HAD.

AND WE GOT NUTS, CRISPS, PISTACHIOS AND SCRATCHINGS - THE LOT!

...SO JENNY TELLS ME YOU TWO ALREADY KNOW EACH OTHER FROM THE LIBRARY!

YOU DO?

...WELL YEAH..! NATURALLY. WHAT WITH HER WORKING THERE AND ME BEING SUCH A BIG READER.

BIG READER?

SURE! HE'S ONE OF OUR BUSIEST READERS AND LIKE ME HE DOES LIKE HIS HISTORY.

TOO RIGHT! THE EGYPTIANS, THE ROMANS, NAPOLEON! I LOVE MY HISTORY DON'T I BRUV?

WELL YEAH...YOU'VE ALWAYS BEEN A BIG FAN...

HE DID WATCH BRAVEHEART A LOT. I REMEMBER THAT.

HE GOT 'NAPOLEON' OUT ON DVD TODAY - THE SIX HOUR FRENCH VERSION.

HE WAS A REAL SMART GUY HE WAS BRUV. YOU SHOULD BORROW IT AFTER.

HMMM...SO AREN'T YOU SUPPOSED TO BE OFF ON THIS 'DEAD IMPORTANT' JOB BY NOW?

OH, I FORGOT ABOUT THAT... WHAT'S THE TIME?

GONE TWELVE.

YOU GOT TO GET OFF THEN?

NAH - SUSPECT THE JOB'S HIT A SNAG. SHOULD HAVE HEARD SOMETHING BY NOW...

ALSO CONCERNED...

TiK-ToK! TiK-ToK! TiK-ToK! TiK-ToK!

YOU THINK HE'S MADE IT THROUGH? WE SHOULD'VE HAD A CALL BY NOW.

THE TRANSPORT'S A GOOD ONE, BUT YOU NEVER CAN TELL.

THE COMFORT INN RESTAURANT...

WHERE THE **FUCK** IS THE MINT SAUCE? GET ME THE WAITRESS!

OKAY BABE. I'LL GET SOME, JUST CALM DOWN...IS SOMETHING WRONG?

NO! EVERYTHING'S JUST FINE... AM EXPECTING A CALL —THAT'S ALL.

TiK! TiK! TiK

AT ROO'S PLACE...

AT LAST! MONTHS OF PATIENCE ARE ABOUT TO PAY OFF...

...THIS IS MY ENTRY INTO THE BIG TIME!

BEEEP! BEEEEP! IT'S TWO O'CLOCK, TIME FOR THE NEWS...

TWO O'CLOCK ALREADY. THIS ISN'T GOOD — NOT GOOD AT ALL...IT'S GETTING LATE!

WHILST AT THE LION.

...AND THEN HIS TROUSERS SPLIT RIGHT UP THE FRONT JUST AS HE...

BRUV! SORT HER OUT WILL YOU...! SHE'S RUINING EVERY-THING...

RIGHT! IT'S OUR ROUND. C'MON BABE — GIVE US A HAND WILL YA.

AND SO...

DON'T YOU 'BABE' ME! GO 'BABE' THAT GIRLFRIEND OF YOURS FROM BEHIND THE BAR!

...GNRRR! SHE'S NOT MY GIRLFRIEND — I DON'T EVEN LIKE HER...

MEANWHILE, SOME -WHERE UP NORTH...

RING! RING!

HIYA. IS THAT YOU CHUCK?

YES. IT'S ME HERE. RUNNING A BIT LATE BUT I'LL BE HOME FOR TEA.

THANK GOD FOR THAT. I'LL RING "EDDIE" AND LET HIM KNOW HIS TEA'S A LITTLE LATE.

SHE THEN RINGS A NUMBER IN SPAIN FROM A MOBILE.

OKAY...ALL IS GOOD. JUST A LITTLE LATE.

PASTILLE JONES RECEIVES THE CALL...

THANK FUCK FOR THAT! WAS THINKING THERE MIGHT BE A PROBLEM.

WHO THEN CALLS BROWNIE...

EXCELLENT! WE'RE IN BUSINESS.

...WHO IN TURN CALLS ROO...

OKAY THEN. WE'LL START GETTING READY.

AND FINALLY...

...OKAY... I'LL GRAB SOME ON THE WAY... MEET YOU IN AN HOUR – THE USUAL PLACE.

YOU GOT TO GO?

YEAH WORK CALLS.

I'D BEST SHOOT OFF. BACK LATER I SHOULD THINK.

I SAID I'D LEND A HAND... THAT'S OKAY ISN'T IT?

...I SUPPOSE SO. JUST DON'T GO CHATTING UP ANY BARMAIDS WHEN YOU'RE OUT...

SO WHAT'S THE PLAN THEN?

I'LL DROP STAN OFF ABOUT FIVE. I'LL THEN GO AND FINISH OFF – BE BACK ABOUT NINE.

WON'T BE LONG...

JUST MAKE SURE TO CALL FIRST. BY NINE WE COULD BE ANYWHERE COULDN'T WE?

WILL DO. RIGHT – WE'RE OFF...

AT A NEARBY TESCO...

YOU MUST BE FUCKING MAD! YOU DON'T NEED THIS.

WELL JUST HEAR ME OUT. IT'S NOT AS DAFT AS IT SEEMS...

LOOK. THE OLD BILL WILL BE LOOKING AT BROWNIE'S BIG NAME LINKS IN THE BIGGER CITIES.

ALLEYTON'S SMALL AND TUCKED AWAY. ME AND ROO ARE LOW PROFILE AND UNDER THE RADAR. WE'RE HIS SAFEST BET.

BUT OUR OWN THING'S GOING WELL. WHY GET INVOLVED IN ALL THIS?

I CAN'T KEEP LOANING OFF YOU TWO. BESIDES, YOU'RE BROKE AN' ALL.

WE'VE THREE WEEKS 'TIL WE HARVEST. THIS JOB WITH ROO'LL KEEP US ALL GOING.

...SO YOU'RE WANTING FIVE OF THESE?

YEAH...THEY'RE CHRISTMAS PRESENTS.

BUT IT'S ONLY AUGUST.

ALL'S PROFESSIONAL ON THIS JOB, BEGINNING WITH CLEAN PHONES. NOW WE'LL GO AND MEET ROO.

PAT'S CAFE ON CLAY LANE...

NO SIGN OF HIS VAN...BET HE'S LATE...

HEY MIKEY. WHERE ARE YOU? ...COURSE, BEEN HERE AGES...

JUST PULLING IN MATE. GET THE TEAS IN.

?

M25. NORTHBOUND. THE SHIPMENT MOVES NORTH...

182 MILES FROM ALLEYTON...

IT'S NOW 15:45.

BACK AT THE LION...

...AND SO THEN HE STARTED GETTING OUT AMERICAN CRIME BOOKS...

I WISH I'D NEVER ASKED..

...THEN AFTER DISCUSSING ITALIAN HISTORY HE GOT VERY INTERESTED IN THE RENAISSANCE...

...OH - MY - GOD! I FORGOT HOW MUCH SHE CAN TALK. I SHOULD CHANGE THE SUBJECT.

...WHICH BY CO-INCIDENCE I LIKE A LOT MYSELF BUT WHICH HE ALSO ENJOYED A...

RIGHT...TIME TO CHANGE THE SUBJECT AND QUICK!

...BUT IT WAS FRENCH THAT SEEMS TO HAVE CAUGHT HIS INTEREST AND WHICH H

AHEM!

YOU WANT TO GO AND WATCH THE FOOTBALL?

I'M NOT SURE. THEY ALWAYS LOSE WHEN I WATCH. HOW ABOUT PLAYING SOME POOL INSTEAD?

EVEN BETTER!

I'LL RACK 'EM UP - YOU CAN BREAK. SO WHY ARE YOU AND STAN NOT TALKING FOR?

GNRRR...WHERE DO I START? ...THEY'VE JUST HIRED A NEW BARMAID HERE AND...

28

TWENTY MINUTES LATER...

...SO SHE'S BEEN GETTING ALL HIS CONDIMENTS READY FOR HIM! CAN YOU BELIEVE THAT?

...GOD KNOWS HOW LONG IT'S BEEN GOING ON!! I MEAN HE GOES IN THERE EVERY...

...SO I SAYS 'WHAT THE FUCK DO YOU THINK YOU'RE DOING?' - 'DO YOU FANCY HER OR WHAT?' AND HE SAYS...

...OH-MY-GOD! SHE CAN TALK. I WISH I'D NEVER ASKED.

NEAR THE CAFE...

...yawn...STILL TIRED I AM. DIDN'T GET ANY SLEEP AT ALL LAST NIGHT.

...NEED MY OWN BED I DO - PLUS I'VE HAD NO BREAKFAST.

WELL, THAT'S JUST THE NATURE OF THE JOB...MMM...

A POLICE TRACKER ON ROO'S CAR MEANS D.S WALKER CAN MONITOR ROO'S CAR FROM A LAPTOP.

...SHOULD BE JUST ALONG HERE.

THAT'S IT! ON YOUR LEFT.

...AND AS EXPECTED IT'S EMPTY.

HE WON'T BE FAR OFF...

CAFE ON THE CORNER. A GOOD CHANCE.

AS STAN IS NOT IN ON THE JOB, HE SITS AWAY FROM MIKEY AND ROO...

...NOW WE'VE EVERYTHING WE NEED EXCEPT WE'RE MISSING THE MOST IMPORTANT THING OF ALL...

MANPOWER! WE NEED TWO OTHERS ON THIS AND TIME'S RUNNING OUT.

YEAH - IT'S A PROBLEM. LET'S GO DOWN THE LIST THEN.

QUIET IN HERE. ...WHERE IS EVERYONE?

IN THE BAR WATCHING THE FOOTY.

MIKEY AND STAN IN THERE?

NO. THEY'RE WORKING.

OH..! ...STRAIGHT WORK IS IT?

YES. OF COURSE!

SHAME. I COULD DO WITH BEING IN ON ONE OF MIKEY'S IDEAS...

?

NOT ONE THAT'D GET US BANGED UP AGAIN OBVIOUSLY BUT JUST A LITTLE SOMETHING THAT WOULD... WHAT??

YOU'VE GOT A BIG MOUTH YOU HAVE!!

WHAT?! WHAT DID I...OH,

A QUICK RECONNAISSANCE...

I'VE CLOCKED HIM.

BACON BAP AND A TEA TO GO PLEASE LUV.

WILL DO LUV.

A SIMPLE LOOKING WRIST WATCH WITH A DIRECTIONAL MICROPHONE AND CAMERA...

...I DUNNO MATE..

IT'S IMAGES ARE TRANSMITTED TO DELTA FOUR PARKED NEARBY.

60 SECONDS LATER...

THAT'LL BE £2.60 LUV.

STREWTH! THAT WAS A BIT QUICK...

...BUT NOT QUICKER THAN ME. THINK I GOT ENOUGH.

I'LL ASK HIM.

OY STAN! HOP OVER HERE A MINUTE.

...HONESTLY. IT WAS SUCH A LONG TIME AGO, AND HE WAS JUST A LAD AT THE TIME.

BUT HE SAID HE WAS NEARLY THIRTY AT THE TIME.

OOPS! I THINK I'M JUST MAKING THINGS WORSE.

YES, BUT HE'S STRAIGHT NOW. DOESN'T DEAL AT ALL ANYMORE. HE'S A REGULAR NINE TILL FIVE GUY NOWADAYS.

BUT THAT'S NOT WHAT HE WAS SUGGESTING.

Y'KNOW, I THINK I'D BEST LEAVE YOU BOTH TO IT — GOT TO GO THE BOG ANYHOW.

...SO IT'S FIVE HUNDRED QUID FOR A FEW HOURS HOURS WORK. WHAT DO YOU SAY?

I DUNNO. WHAT DO YOU THINK BRUV?

HE'S RIGHT IN WHAT HE SAYS. WE ARE AWAY FROM THE HEAT. IT'S LOW RISK AND THE MONEY'S GOOD.

BUT IT'S YOUR DECISION BRUV.

SO THIS JOB THEY'RE ON... IT'S NOTHING DODGY AT ALL THEN?

OF COURSE NOT. IT'S HIS REGULAR JOB. HE DOES THEM ALL THE TIME.

SO ARE YOU IN THEN?

IT'S UP TO YOU BRUV.

I...ER...

WELL THAT'S A RELIEF. I WAS THINKING IT WAS ALL LOOKING A LITTLE SUSPECT THE WAY THEY SHOT OFF AND THAT THEY WERE UP TO...

NO, NO, NO! THEY'LL BE OFF FITTING SOME LOCKS SOMEWHERE. IT'S NOTHING DODGY AT ALL.

BESIDES, I KNOW MY STAN AND HE WOULD NO WAY GET MIXED UP IN ANYTHING ILLEGAL — HE HAS FAR TOO MUCH SENSE.

SOUNDS GOOD. **I'M IN!**

DOWN THE ROAD...

BRILLIANT WORK MATE. BY THE WAY DID YOU GRAB ME SOME FOOD AN' ALL?

OH...ERM WELL I...

YOU' TELLING ME YOU DIDN'T BRING ME BACK ANYTHING?

NO. I STAYED IN CHARACTER AND JUST GOT MY OWN.

BLOODY HELL! I'VE NOT EATEN SINCE LAST NIGHT.

I'D SAVE YOU SOME BUT I'VE BITTEN INTO IT NOW...

LET'S SEE WHAT WE'VE GOT THEN.

sigh... HERE IT IS. I'VE SENT IT IN ALREADY, THEY'VE GOT STRAIGHT BACK...

DUNNO MATE...YOU ANY IDEAS?

...CONFIRMED THIS GUY IS 'ROO SMITH'; AN UP AND COMING DEALER SO FAR UNTOUCHED, BUT NOT UNKNOWN TO US.

NICE ONE.

AS FOR THE OTHER FELLA, THEY'RE RUNNING CHECKS ON HIM RIGHT NOW. THEY'LL HAVE SOME-THING SOON I EXPECT.

SO WE'RE CLEAR ON HOW WE'RE DOING THIS? FRESH PHONES, FRESH MOTORS. - I SORT OUT THE YARD, YOU GET HOLD OF COZ.

ALL'S CLEAR AS A BELL.

GOOD TO HAVE YOU ON BOARD STAN. DO AS MIKEY SAYS AND IT'LL RUN LIKE CLOCKWORK.

I'LL GET THESE PHONES ON AND START CHECKING IN EVERY TWENTY MINUTES.

MPH! 'SOUNDS GOOD!' 'I'M IN!' - WHAT WE'RE YOU THINKING? Y'KNOW THIS COULD BE DANGEROUS?

BUT YOU DO NEED PEOPLE YOU CAN TRUST!

WE DO. BUT THESE THINGS CAN BE RISKY AND... sigh... I SEE YOUR POINT.

IT'S MUCH LESS RISKY WORKING WITH FAMILY. YOU'VE BEEN TELLING ME FOR WEEKS NOW.

YEAH - ALRIGHT. I GET YOUR POINT. 'WORKING WITH FAMILY' IS THE SAFEST THING. BUT THIS IS A ONE OFF BRUV. YOU CAN'T BE MAKING A HABIT OUT OF IT-GOT IT?!

SOCA'S MIDLAND'S H.Q: HOME OF OPERATION ROULETTE...

ANYTHING NEW WALKER? TIME'S TICKING YOU KNOW.

...WE'VE GOT THE CASINO GUY'S SECOND CONTRACT PHONE PINPOINTED AND ITS CALLS INTERCEPTED.

INFO FROM T-MOBILE PINPOINTS HIM AS STOPPING AT A COMFORT INN NEAR THE TOWN OF ALLEYTON...

...FROM WHERE OUR INTERCEPTS HAVE RECORDED ELEVEN CALLS SINCE LAST NIGHT TO A GUY NAMED 'ROO'...

ROO, JUST DON'T LET ME DOWN, THERE'S A LOT RIDING ON THIS ONE...

...WE'VE NOW PINPOINTED THIS ROO'S PHONE TO 176 WARWICK AVENUE, ALLEYTON AND PUT UNIT DELTA FOUR ON HIM...

...WHO JUST AN HOUR AGO SENT US THIS VIDEO CLIP FROM A LOCAL CAFE WHERE HE MEETS THIS SECOND MAN..

...THIS ISN'T REALLY HIS SORT OF THING...

I'M GUESSING FROM YOUR TONE YOU'VE PUT HIS PICTURE THROUGH THE SYSTEM AND KNOW WHO THIS MAN IS?

COURSE SIR. NAME IS MICHAEL LIONEL JOHNSON. I'LL PULL OUT HIS FILE.

ROO STEPS UP HIS PREPARATION.

FIRSTLY HE GARAGES HIS EVERY-DAY CAR THAT'S REGISTERED IN HIS OWN NAME.

HE THEN WALKS FIFTY YARDS TO ANOTHER GARAGE...

...AND TAKES OUT HIS WORKS CAR THAT'S REGISTERED TO SOMEONE ELSE.

...HE THEN SORTS OUT HIS NEW PHONES...

...SETTING UP HIS NEW PAY-AS-YOU-GO PHONES FOR THE FUTURE GRAFT.

THE FIRST IS A DIRECT LINE TO CASINO OWNER BROWNIE...

...THIS IS MY NEW NUMBER FOR THE DAY... YEAH, ALL'S GOING WELL HERE.

...AND THE SECOND A DIRECT LINE TO MIKEY AND THE WORKERS.

...AM ON MY WAY... WELL KEEP TRYING HIM UNTIL HE ANSWERS.

THE THIRD WILL LATER LINK HIM TO THE LORRY DRIVER.

NATIONAL VAN HIRE IN NEARBY BYWORTH...

COZ IS STILL ENGAGED. WHAT YOU DOING?

JUST TEXTING THE GIRLS. LETTING 'EM KNOW I'LL BE COMING BACK WITH YOU LATER.

GOOD IDEA. ASK IF COZ IS THERE? HE'S USUALLY IN THE LION ON A SATURDAY...

NOW YOU JUST WAIT OUT HERE.

AFTERNOON SIR... MISTER ROBERTS ISN'T IT?

THAT'S RIGHT. JUST WANTING TO RENT A VAN FOR A FEW DAYS.

STILL ENGAGED...

YEAH...BLACKBALL ...I'M WORKING ON IT RIGHT NOW...

...ONCE I'VE GOT SOMETHING I'LL LET YOU KNOW AND WE CAN MEET UP.

WELL YOU'LL JUST HAVE TO WAIT. I CAN'T RUSH THESE THINGS.

...JUST GIVE ME MY SPACE AND STOP CALLING. I'LL CALL YOU WHEN I HAVE SOME...EH?

AHEM!

...WE'RE STILL WAITING FOR YOU TO TAKE YOUR SHOT!

OH...! SOZ ABOUT THAT.

BLOODY CUSTOMERS. SOMEONE ALWAYS WANTING SOMETHING.

DIDN'T THINK YOU WERE DEALING ANY-MORE.

I'M NOT. BUT SOME PEOPLE JUST WON'T TAKE NO FOR AN ANSWER.

BEEEP!

MMPH!...IT'S FROM MY IDIOT BOYFRIEND...

...il NOKIA
WORKING WITH M. BACK AT 9. IS COZ IN? NEED 2 SPEAK 2 HIM.
Options | Back

...SAYS HE'S WORKING UNTIL NINE, SAYS HE NEEDS TO SPEAK TO YOU COZ.

SPEAK TO ME?

THAT'S WHAT IT SAYS.

OH. I'LL RING HIM THEN.

...NEXT THING IS A CHANGE OF CLOTHES. SOMETHING MORE SUITED TO NIGHT WORK.

YOU MEAN WE GET TO DRESS ALL IN BLACK?

NATIONAL VAN HIRE

NO, NO! THIS AIN'T THE MOVIES BRUV. JUST SOME DARK CLOTHES 'LL DO.

OH..!

RING! RING!

'BIT OF LUCK, THAT'LL BE COZ.

YEAH... HE'S HERE... I'LL PASS HIM ON.

IS KAYE LISTENING?

OF COURSE.

JUST LISTEN THEN.

A MINUTE LATER.

SO YOU INTERESTED THEN?

YEAH. I'LL HELP.

...THOSE FIRE DOORS ARE HEAVY BUGGERS. THREE OF US WILL MANAGE IT FINE. I'LL GRAB SOME TOOLS AND BE RIGHT OVER.

I'LL SEE YOU AT MAC'S PLACE.

BE THERE AS SOON AS I CAN.

GOT TO GO LADIES – LOVE YA AND LEAVE YA.

IN YOUR DREAMS.

SEE YA.

WORKING ON A WEEKEND. SUCH HARD WORKERS.

...OR SUCH BIG LIARS!

CRADLED IN THE WOODS BEHIND ALLEYTON LIBRARY LIES ROO'S OLD SCRAPYARD.

HIYA FELLAS!

BARK! BARK!

BARK, BARK BARK!

NOW ITS SOLE OCCUPANTS ARE GUARD DOGS 'ABBOT AND COSTELLO'...

...YEAH!...WE'VE WORK TONIGHT...OH YEAH...DADDY'S GONNA MAKE A FORTUNE...

YELP! YELP! YELP!

ELSEWHERE...

OH BUGGER ME! HE MUST'VE SWITCHED VEHICLES.

NOT AS DUMB AS THEY SEEM IF YOU ASK ME.

...YES SIR. JUST LOST 'TARGET 2'...

...HE'S SWITCHED VEHICLES... YES SIR... THEY DO SEEM TO KNOW WHAT THEY'RE DOING AFTER ALL!

HE FEEDS THE DOGS AND HEADS OFF FOR THE OFFICE...

...NOT AN IDEAL CHOICE, BUT FOR ONE NIGHT ONLY IT'LL DO THE JOB.

CHOMP! CHOMP! CHOMP!

HE RINGS BROWNIE...

YEAH MATE, ALL'S GOING WELL HERE.

...BUT I'M NOW NEEDING A NUMBER FOR YOUR DRIVER SO I CAN LINK UP...

...ALSO, I NEED TO KNOW EXACTLY WHERE THE CHAMPAGNE* IS PLACED.

...THAT'S GOOD - JUST FINE...NO... NONE OF THEM KNOW ANYTHING ABOUT IT YET...

FUCK! IF I TOLD THE BIG LAD HE'D HAVE A FIT. HE'S A BIT OLD FASHIONED THESE DAYS.

...YEAH... I'LL HAVE TO TELL HIM LATER ON, BUT BY THEN IT'LL BE TOO LATE FOR HIM TO BACK OUT.

* CHAMPAGNE - COCAINE

AT MAC'S PLACE.

...FOOD'S ALL CRAP AT THESE PLACES. ALL SALT, SUGAR AND FATS. I DON'T KNOW HOW THEY GET AWAY WITH IT.

YOU NOT HAVING ANY THEN? IT IS MY ROUND.

COURSE I AM. I'M STARVED! BIG MAC MEAL 'LL DO ME.

JUST TWO BIG MAC MEALS THEN.

OH! AND GET ME A FLURRY. I LOVE THEM FLURRIES...

...AND A KIDDIE MEAL - WITH NUGGETS AND STRAWBERRY SHAKE, WITH ONE OF THEM TOY THINGS.

...BUT MAKE SURE IT'S NOT THE LION AGAIN - I'VE GOT TWO OF THEM ALREADY...

YOU HAVEN'T GOT THE PANDA HAVE YOU?

sigh...! AND THAT'S IT IS IT?

YEAH... IT'LL DO I SUPPOSE.

WOULD YOU ORDER THE FOOD WHILST I JUST NIP THE LOO?

OF COURSE.

...NOW TO FIND OUT WHAT THE FUCK'S GOING ON!!

'ON A JOB'? WORKING UNTIL NINE ON A SUNDAY! HOW STUPID DO THEY THINK I AM?

WOMEN

GNRRR! THE TRUTH I CAN HANDLE. IT'S BEING LIED TO I CAN'T STAND!!

...IF THEY'RE UP TO SOMETHING THEN HE SHOULD HAVE TOLD ME. I MEAN, I'M A REASONABLE PERSON.

GNRRRR! BUT IF HE IS UP TO SOMETHING THEN GOD HELP HIM!!

THIS IS GOING TO HAVE TO BE SHORT AND SWEET.

THEY'RE EXPECTING ME AT MAC'S PLACE ANYTIME NOW. TIME'S SHORT.

LET'S GET TO IT THEN.

OKAY. IT'S ARRIVING IN SOMETIME BETWEEN SIX AND EIGHT TONIGHT.

AND THE PLAYERS ARE?

ROO'S IN CHARGE. ME, MIKEY AND HIS KID BROTHER ARE THE WORKERS.

AND HOW MUCH IS COMING IN?

DUNNO. BUT KNOWING ROO AND THE CASINO GUY IT WON'T JUST BE THE OLD WEED...

NO?

NO?

COURSE NOT. THERE'LL BE SOME 'EXPENSIVE' ON AN'ALL. Y'KNOW, THE 'POWDER', THE 'CHARLIE'—THE OLD 'COCAINE'!

...AND YOU'RE SURE ON THAT?

COURSE I AM. I GET MINE OFF ROO, HE GET'S HIS OFF THE CASINO GUY. MARK MY WORDS, IT'LL BE IN THERE SOMEWHERE.

MMMM...AND WHERE'S THIS ALL COMING INTO? WHAT'S YOUR LOCATION?

I DUNNO YET I'LL KNOW THAT ONCE I'VE LINKED UP WITH THE OTHERS.

HAVEN'T YOU GOT ANY IDEA?

IT IS THE MOST IMPORTANT PART.

LET ME THINK...

YEAH - I'LL MEET YOU AT THE SERVICES.

...HE DOES HAVE A FEW PLACES DOTTED ABOUT.

WELL PUT YOUR FOOT DOWN. WE'RE ALL READY AND WAITING.

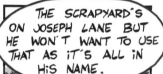

HE'S A FEW GARAGES AND HIS OLD SCRAPYARD, PLUS CASINO GUY 'LL HAVE SOME PLACES...

AND..?

YEAH..!

ROO'S GARAGES ARE NEAR THE STATION, BEHIND WARREN STREET. REAL GOOD PLACES TO LEAVE GEAR OVERNIGHT...

THE SCRAPYARD'S ON JOSEPH LANE BUT HE WON'T WANT TO USE THAT AS IT'S ALL IN HIS NAME.

SO JUST WHERE DO *YOU* THINK HE'LL BE TAKING IT TO?

DUNNO. BUT I'LL KNOW AS SOON AS I GET TO MAC'S PLACE.

I'M GONNA HAVE TO SHOOT. AS SOON AS I KNOW WHERE I'LL CALL IT IN. BE ABOUT HALF AN HOUR.

YOU THINK THIS SCUMBAG WILL FIND OUT WHERE?

HE'D BETTER. WITHOUT KNOWING THEIR LOCATION WE'RE GOING TO HAVE A MASSIVE PROBLEM.

17:15: ARRIVING ON THE M1 NORTH...

108 MILES TO ALLEYTON.

WAITING FOR COZ.

I KNEW WE SHOULDN'T HAVE ASKED HIM!

HE'S USUALLY LATE THOUGH ISN'T HE?

HMPH! NEVER USED TO BE. ALWAYS USED TO BE ON TIME HE DID BUT...

sigh... HE'S GOT ALL SLOPPY AND AMATEURISH LATELY...

?

FOREVER GETTING PISSED, NOT ANSWERING HIS PHONE, LYING IN BED ALL DAY...

CLICK!

♪SEX BOMB! SEX BOMB! ♪YOU'RE MY SEXBOMB AND B...♪

HEY LOOK! HERE HE IS...

IS YOURS NO GOOD THEN?

...AM JUST NOT HUNGRY.

OH.

LOOK KAYE, CAN I BE STRAIGHT WITH YOU?

COURSE.

SOMETHING'S CLEARLY BOTHERING YOU. IS THERE SOMETHING WRONG?

YOU CAN TELL ME YOU KNOW! WE'VE KNOWN EACH OTHER FOR YEARS NOW...

...AND I'M NOT EASILY SHOCKED.

ER, WELL...

ONE MINUTE LATER.

BLOODY HELL! A DRUGS FACTORY!

SHSHSHSH!

THE WHITE LION

? ? ? ?

...AND SO HOW LONG HAS THIS BEEN GOING ON FOR?

JUST A COUPLE OF MONTHS.

STREWTH! AND SO NOW YOU THINK THAT...

THIS NEIGHBOUR'S RUNG THE OLD BILL AND NOW STAN, COZ AND MIKEY ARE CLEAR-ING IT OUT BEFORE IT'S RAIDED!

MMMM, NO WONDER YOU'RE WORRIED. WHY NOT CALL STAN AND FIND OUT WHAT'S GOING ON.

I HAVE. BUT HE JUST LIED TO ME!!

OH...! AND STAN LOOKS SO HONEST AS WELL.

I KNOW! I'LL RING MIKEY. HE'D NEVER LIE TO ME!

BRILLIANT!

RING!

HELLO..! NO IT'S MIKEY. WHO'S - OH, IT'S YOU.

SHE SAID WHAT? MMM...OH...! OF COURSE WE'RE NOT UP TO ANYTHING.

SHE IS?... WELL THERE'S NO NEED.

THEY'RE WITH ME NOW... HONESTLY! JUST LISTEN...

SAY 'HI' YOU TWO.

HI!

HI!

Y'SEE? WE'RE JUST FITTING THE FIRST DOOR NOW. WITH COZ HERE IT WON'T TAKE US LONG.

YEAH...OKAY THEN. WE'LL SEE YOU ABOUT NINE, TEN AT THE LATEST. YOU'LL STILL BE THERE WON'T YOU?

AAHH GOOD! LATER THEN... BYE...SEE YA...!

YEAH...SEE YA!

YOU'RE RIGHT. HE'S LYING. THEY'RE CLEARLY UP TO SOMETHING.

SEE! I TOLD YA?

AND THAT'S HOW YOU HANDLE 'EM. JUST GOTTA GIVE THEM A LITTLE REASSURANCE.

THAT'S RIGHT. OTHERWISE THEY'LL ALWAYS BE WORRYING ABOUT NOTHING.

WORRYING ABOUT NOTHING?

RIGHT YOU LOT. WE'RE ABOUT TO TURN THIS OPERATION AROUND!

THE CONFERENCE ROOM AT ALLEYTON CENTRAL POLICE STATION...

TWO NIGHTS AGO WE JUMPED IN TOO SOON. TONIGHT, WE WILL NOT BE MAKING THE SAME MISTAKE!

BY SIX THIRTY WE WILL HAVE ALL THE DATA REQUIRED ON THE LOCATIONS TO BE HIT. WE WILL THEN BE MOVING DOUBLE QUICK.

OUTSIDE, ALL IS ON STANDBY...

DETECTIVE CHIEF SUPERINTENDENT'S OFFICE.

...I DO FEEL SURE HE'LL BE IN TOUCH SOON. HE'S ONE OF OUR VERY BEST INFORMANTS SIR.

I HOPE YOU'RE RIGHT. WE'RE FAST RUNNING OUT OF TIME.

NOW LET'S HAVE A QUICK RUN DOWN OF WHAT'S HAPPENING.

D.S GAUNT

ALPHA ONE HAS CHECKED OUT THE GARAGES BY THE STATION, BUT SO FAR NO SIGNS OF ACTIVITY.

UNIT SIX HAS EYEBALLED THE SCRAPYARD. A WHITE MALE AND A FORD MONDEO WERE SIGHTED.

RAN A CHECK ON THE MONDEO; REGISTERED TO AN UNOCCUPIED FLAT IN NORTH ALLEYTON.

D.S. ROBERTS

TARGET 1: BROWNIE PRICE AKA 'CASINO GUY, HIS MOBILE STILL HAS HIM PINPOINTED TO A LOCAL HOTEL.

OUR ENQUIRIES CONFIRM THAT HE'S CHECKED INTO ROOM 12 ON THE GROUND FLOOR.

WE'VE A TEN MAN TEAM POSITIONED NEARBY, READY TO GO IN AT A MOMENT'S NOTICE.

D.S JONES

STILL NO NEWS ON TARGET 2: ROO SMITH. WE'RE CERTAIN HE'S SWITCHED VEHICLES AND PHONES.

XT5687

Flat 6
Apollo Ho...
MICHAEL JOHNSON
11/11/77

RJ1842

BETTER NEWS WITH TARGET 3: MICHAEL JOHNSON. THE IDIOT'S CARRYING HIS WORK'S MOBILE ON HIM.

INFO FROM VODAPHONE HAS HAD HIM POSITIONED AT A NEARBY McDONALDS THIS LAST HOUR. HE MUST BE JUST WAITING NOW.

49

OKAY. I'LL GO THROUGH THIS THE ONCE. SAVE YOUR QUESTIONS FOR AFTER.

SO THIS IS HOW TONIGHT 'LL PAN OUT.

ROO'S ALREADY GONE OUT TO THE SERVICES TO MEET THE DRIVER.

ONCE HE'S LINKED UP HE'LL SUSS OUT ALL'S STRAIGHT AND GOOD.

BACK IN ABOUT TWO HOURS.

ALL'S CLEAR BEHIND. SWEET AS A NUT.

ONCE HAPPY, HE'LL GRAB THE TRANSPORT AND GET MOVING.

HE'LL THEN GIVE US A CALL...

BABY'LL BE DELIVERED IN 20 MINUTES.

AND WE'LL GET GOING.

LOOK FORWARD TO IT MATE.

WE THEN HEAD FOR THE YARD, BEING DOUBLY CARE-FUL NO-ONE'S ON US.

NOW KEEP YOUR EYES PEELED.

THE GEAR'LL BE GOING TO ROO'S OLD SCRAPYARD DOWN JOSEPH LANE...

IT'S NICE AND PRIVATE, PLUS HE'S GOT THE DOGS.

JUST DON'T LET 'EM KNOW YOU'RE SCARED.

'COZ THEY CAN CAN SMELL FEAR.

GRRRR!

AND ALSO HE'S GOT STORAGE CONTAINERS WHICH ARE IDEAL.

ROO THEN ARRIVES...

BARK! BARK! BARK! BARK!

WE OPEN UP THE LORRY AND FIND THE GEAR...

AND THEN OFFLOAD AS QUICK AS WE CAN.

THE GEAR GOES INTO ONE OF THE CONTAINERS...

ROO'LL BE OUT ON WATCH DURING THIS.

ONCE UNLOADED, ROO WILL RETURN THE LORRY BACK TO THE DRIVER.

IT'LL BE OUR JOB TO LOCK UP AND SECURE THE PLACE.

THEN, WE SIMPLY GET THE FUCK OUT OF THERE!

BE DONE AND DUSTED IN NINETY MINUTES. ANY QUESTIONS?

HOW COME HE'S USING HIS OWN PLACE? I THOUGHT HE'D HAVE GOT A NEW PLACE.

NO CHOICE. HE'S HAD NO TIME TO GET ANYWHERE ELSE. THIS WILL DO THOUGH.

I SUPPOSE SO.

ROO'S CONFIDENT IT'LL ONLY BE THERE FOR A FEW DAYS ANYHOW.

18:45: HEADING NORTH ON THE M1...

Services 16m

32 MILES TO ALLEYTON

ALREADY WAITING AT LEICESTER FOREST SERVICES.

ALL SET THEN. SHOULDN'T BE LONG NOW.

NOW LET'S RECAP ON WHAT'S COMING IN.

THREE TON' OF WEED AND FIFTY KILOS OF COKE...!

WE ALL KNOW IT'S THE COKE WHERE THE REAL MONEY IS...

AT LAST!

SAFE TO SAFE, I'M FINALLY IN THE BIG TIME NOW.

ELSEWHERE...

I'M NIPPING IN TO USE THEIR BOG. ANYONE WANT ANYTHING?

I'M GOOD.

NO TA.

GOOD TO GET OUT OF THERE...

52

COZ'S INFO IS PASSED ON...

...THE SCRAPYARD ON JOSEPH LANE...THE DRIVER'S BEING MET NOW — RIGHT, WE'RE ON IT.

OKAY GENTLEMEN. TIME TO GET DOWN TO BUSINESS!

ELSEWHERE.

HI THERE MATE. AM ONE MINUTE AWAY. I'LL BE SEEING YOU IN A FEW MINUTES.

NOW, I'M A SHORT TUBBY GUY, A LITTLE THIN ON TOP. WHAT ABOUT YOU? HOW DO I RECOGNISE YOU?

I'M THE TALL HANDSOME GUY IN A WHITE T-SHIRT; GOT A GOOD SET OF HAIR. YOU CAN'T MISS ME.

UNITS MOVE!

HE'S DOING THE PICK UP NOW. WE'VE LESS THAN THIRTY MINUTES.

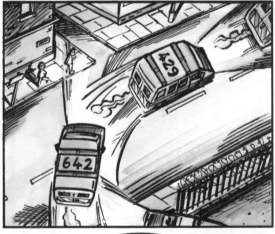

...FIT HANDSOME GUY ON THE EDGE OF THE CAR PARK? YOU MUST'VE SEEN ME.

I SEE YOU NOW.

...LEAVE IT WITH ME FOR A COUPLE OF HOURS. YOU JUST SIT TIGHT.

HERE WE GO THEN...! IT'S PARTY TIME...

FLASH BUGGER! ..SUPPOSE HE IS HANDSOME THOUGH.

POLICE AIR SUPPORT UNIT...

SO FAR, SO GOOD. NOW TO KEEP YOUR WITS ABOUT YOU...

THAT FAT LITTLE LORRY DRIVER WOULD BE CLUELESS IF ANY-ONE WAS FOLLOWING HIM...

...MIND YOU, IT'S VERY DIFFICULT TO TELL. BEST GET ONTO THOSE BACKROADS.

TWO DOG UNITS - FOUR OFFICERS.

FIVE POLICE VANS - SIXTY OFFICERS.

ONE ARMED RESPONSE UNIT - TWENTY OFFICERS.

ROO TURNS OFF THE M1 AND ONTO QUIETER BACKROADS.

NOTHING'S COME WITH ME... GOOD AND CLEAR!

TIME TO GIVE MIKEY A CALL...ALL'S GOING TO PLAN.

COZ PLACES THEIR PERSONAL MOBILES IN HIS CAR...

SO WHY ARE WE LEAVING OUR MOBILES HERE FOR?

NOTHING TO WORRY ABOUT BRUV. IT'S THE NORMAL THING TO DO.

OH, I SEE.

CAN'T HAVE 'OLD BILL' TRACKING OUR MOBILES. YOU JUST NEVER KNOW.

PLUS THEY CAN ACTIVATE MOBILES AS BUGS NOW.*¹ IT'S REAL SMART SHIT.

?

HEY, QUIET NOW... HERE'S OUR CALL. HI MATE...CAN WE MOVE NOW?

FUCK ME THIS IS ALL GETTING A BIT SERIOUS!

SO HOW ON EARTH DID YOU END UP GETTING INVOLVED IN ALL THIS ANYHOW?

WOMEN

...I'M AFRAID IT'S A LONG STORY AND I'M SWORN TO SECRECY...

...THOUGH IT WAS A WHILE AGO NOW... SO I COULD... NO..! SOME -THINGS ARE MEANT TO STAY SECRET...

...I COULDN'T POSSIBLY SAY...

OH.

IT ALL STARTED LAST YEAR WHEN WE WENT ON THIS HOLIDAY TO SPAIN...*²

*¹ ROVING BUGS: COMING TO A COURT NEAR YOU.
*² SEE BOOK I: 'HIM & HER'S SMUGGLING VACATION'

56

... NO ... NOTHING'S WITH ME, I'M ALL CLEAN. HOW ABOUT YOU, ANYTHING WITH YOU?

GOOD, GOOD. I'LL BE ABOUT FIFTEEN MINUTES MYSELF.

OPPOSITE THE SCRAPYARD RUNS A LONE JOGGER...

BARK! BARK!

BARK! BARK! BARK!

... EXHAUSTED, HE STOPS FOR A BRIEF REST...

Huff...puff ...huff...

BEFORE SWIFTLY JOGGING AWAY...

...HE LEAVES BEHIND A SMALL CAMERA THE SIZE OF A LIGHTER.

POLICE UNITS ARRIVE AT THEIR DESIGNATED POSITIONS...

...ON WASTELAND, HOTEL CAR PARKS, BUSINESS PARKS...

...ALL WITHIN TWO MINUTES DRIVE OF THE SCRAPYARD.

THREE MILES TO GO...

THIS IS ALL GOING TOO WELL...

STONE ME!

THERE'S NO GOING BACK NOW...

MEANWHILE, KAYE SPILLS ALL ON LAST YEAR'S SPANISH ADVENTURE...

...AND THEIR ATTEMPT AT DRUG SMUGGLING...

...THE JOURNEY UP SPAIN AND FRANCE...

...AND THE DISASTER THAT STRUCK THEM AT THE ELEVENTH HOUR...

...AND THAT'S HOW WE LOST IT. JUST ONE OF THOSE THINGS I GUESS!

...!

YOU OKAY?

...I'M JUST TAKING IT ALL IN—CHRIST! YOU MUST'VE BEEN OUT OF YOUR MINDS! I MEAN—

IF YOU'D GOT CAUGHT YOU'D'VE GONE TO PRISON!

BUT IF WE'D GOT AWAY WITH IT WE'D HAVE BEEN RICH NOW!

...YES, BUT IF YOU'D.... I SUPPOSE YOU'VE GOT A POINT...

YOUR WINE...!

THERE YOU GO LADIES.

THANKS.

Hmph! grumble 'THANKS' ...mutter...

ENJOY.

HMPH! DID YOU SEE THAT? GNRRrrr! THAT GIRL'S GOT SUCH AN ATTITUDE ON HER!

TWO MILES TO GO...

SO SERIOUS...

...SHOULD'VE STAYED AT HOME...

...I'LL NEVER MAKE THIS MISTAKE AGAIN!..

BACK AT THE LION...

OOops! MISSED IT AGAIN... I'LL JUST PUT IT BACK

OOooo...THIS WINE'S QUITE STRONG..!

IT'S THIRTEEN PER CENT THAT ONE IS..!

TASTES LIKE IT...AND LOOKS LIKE IT.

RIGHT. THIS TIME I'LL CLIP THE NICE RED BUT MISS THAT NASTY BLACKBALL!

NOW CONCENTRATE! CLIP THE REDBALL. MISS THE BLACKBALL. ...ONE MINUTE THOUGH...

YOU TAKING IT THEN?

...'BLACKBALL' - THAT WAS THE NAME COZ WAS SPEAK-ING TO EARLIER...

... AND THEN LAST YEAR AT CUSTOMS YOU OVERHEARD...

THAT WAS IT WASN'T IT...?

YOU ALRIGHT KAYE? IS THERE SOMETHING WRONG?

NINE MONTHS EARLIER...

...THE ...ENED?

NOTHING!

AWFUL INTELLIGENCE IF YOU ASK ME...

IT WAS OFF A RELIABLE SOURCE. ONE OF THE BEST!

BLACKBALL'S BEEN SPOT ON EVERY TIME - UP UNTIL NOW THAT IS...

?

...UP - GR... JUST GRE...

THEY SAID 'BLACKBALL'! I'M SURE IT WAS, AND THEN EARLIER...

YEAH...BLACKBALL ...I'M WORKING ON IT RIGHT NOW...

... ONCE I'VE GOT SOMETHING I'LL LET YOU KNOW AND WE CAN MEET UP.

KAYE!

THE ARIEL UNIT ARRIVES IN POSITION.

DUM! DUM! DUM! DUM!

STAYING DOWNWIND FROM THE LOCATION TO BE RAIDED...

DUM! DUM! DUM! DUM! DUM!

...MEANS THE SOUND OF ITS BLADES CANNOT BE HEARD FROM THE SCRAPYARD.

BACK ON THE GROUND...

ARE YOU THERE YET? I'M ONLY FIVE MINUTES AWAY MYSELF.

JUST TURNING ONTO THE LANE NOW. BE THERE IN SIXTY SECONDS.

THINGS TO REMEMBER...

FIRSTLY: IT'S ONLY ONCE I CAN SEE THE GEAR THAT I TAKE MY JACKET OFF...

...ON SEEING THAT, THEY'RE COMING IN FAST, LOUD AND HARD.

...THINK I'LL SPOT THEM FIRST. I'LL SHOUT A WARNING 'THEY'RE ON US!'

TOO LATE FOR THEM! TO RUN. THEY'VE HAD IT. GONE! FINISHED!

GAME OVER!

POLICE UNITS NOW IN THEIR POSITIONS...

ALL WITHIN A MILE AND A HALF OF THE TARGET...

ALL READY TO GO IN.

NOW THEY WAIT...

AND WAIT...

...AND WAIT.

JUST ONE MILE TO GO.

...A GRAND FOR A NIGHTS WORK SEEMS A LOT...

...BUT IF YOU GET NICKED, IT'S FUCK ALL REALLY!

Sigh...! THIS IS NO SORT OF LIFE.

I MEAN, YOU'RE RISKING WHAT LITTLE YOU HAVE BY BEING HERE!

AS FOR HIM! HE WOULDN'T EVEN BE HERE IF IT WASN'T FOR YOU...

...YOU KNOW WHAT YOU'VE GOT TO DO..!

THE FIRST ARRIVAL...

HERE WE GO THEN...

WE'VE SEEN IT. MAINTAIN RADIO SILENCE UNTIL WE GET THE SIGNAL.

OUT IN THE FIELD...

C'MON...! WE'RE ALL SET HERE.

THIS IS WHAT IT'S ALL ABOUT —CATCHING THE BAD GUYS.

I DO HOPE THERE'S SOME AGGRO!

GONNA CRACK ME SOME SKULLS!

C'MON YOU FUCKERS!

...GIVE US THE SIGNAL!

TURN YOUR LIGHTS DOWN WILL YA!! FOR FUCK'S SAKE...!

BARK! BARK! BARK!

...DON'T WANT THE WHOLE NEIGHBOURHOOD SEEING WE'RE ABOUT...

HIYA YOU PAIR...YEAH...IT'S GOOD TO SEE YOU TOO...

...I'M GONNA HAVE A QUICK MOOCH UP THE TOP. YOU GRAB THE HANDSCANNER AND GIVE THAT CARAVAN A QUICK CHECK OVER. —BE BACK IN TWO MINS.

...I CAN'T BELIEVE HE DUMPED ME OUT LIKE THAT...!

...IF I WASN'T SO RELIEVED I'D BE ANGRY.

...WONDER WHAT MADE HIM ACT LIKE THAT THOUGH...

...UNLESS HE THOUGHT I WASN'T UP TO IT, IN WHICH CASE...

...HE WAS RIGHT.

...AT LEAST IT'S ONLY A FIVE MINUTE WALK TO THE PUB.

ROO ARRIVES...

...JUST WATCH HER AS YOU COME IN...

YEAH...LOADS OF SPACE...SWING HER AROUND...

HERE WE GO THEN...

...BEST PLAY THE PART AS CONVINCINGLY AS I CAN.

...THIS WAY ROO... OVER TO THIS ONE.

69

WHAT DO YOU MEAN HE'S NOT WITH YOU?

WHERE IS HE THEN?

HOLD ON! I THOUGHT YOU WERE PLEASED TO SEE ME!

I AM!

SHE IS!!

SO WHERE IS HE?

YES! WHERE IS HE?

HE'S STILL OUT WORKING WITH COZ OF COURSE.

WITH COZ!!!

YEAH, WITH COZ. WHAT'S UP?

Y'KNOW, HE'S NOT GOING TO BELIEVE THIS.

WELL YOU HAVE TO TELL HIM.

TELL ME WHAT?

ONE MINUTE LATER...

'BLACKBALL'!

THAT'S THE NAME HE USED.

BUT 'COZ'! A POLICE INFORMANT? THERE MUST BE ANOTHER REASON.

SUCH AS WHAT?

I DON'T KNOW, BUT HE COULDN'T BE — MIKEY'S KNOWN HIM FOR YEARS.

72

ARE THEY REALLY ON A DOOR JOB? THEY'RE NOT ARE THEY?

I CAN'T REALLY SAY...NO, I...

YOU HAVE TO... WE NEED TO KNOW!

C'MON STAN! THIS IS IMPORTANT.

STANLEY. IT'S TIME TO TELL THE TRUTH.

BUT I CAN'T, MIKEY'LL...

I'LL ASK YOU ONE MORE TIME; AND DON'T LIE TO ME.

...YOU KNOW I CAN TELL WHEN YOU'RE LYING.

AND SO...

ALRIGHT! I'M RINGING HIM NOW.

JUST HOW STUPID CAN YOU BE?!!

EVERYTHING'S GOING TO BE ALRIGHT ISN'T IT?

OY!

BLOODY OLD BILL ARE DOWN THE ROAD!

EXIT

...HE ONLY PUT IT ON A FEW HOURS AGO — HE SHOULD BE ANSWERING...

I HOPE SO... — sigh!...HEY, WHAT'S GOING ON?

SOMETHING OUTSIDE...

POLICE DOWN THE ROAD...

HOPE IT'S A MURDER OR SOMETHING.

LIGHTS EVERYWHERE!

EXIT

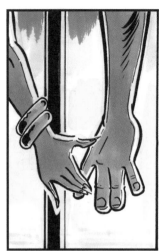

WHAT A STUPID THING TO DO..!

SO SILLY MIKEY...

...SO BLOODY SILLY.

THE END.

SMUGGLING VACATION

The book that kicked it all off. The controversial and acclaimed
adventure of two Brits abroad who became drug smugglers.

Available from www.smugglingvacation.co.uk